EDGE BOOKS™

RECREATIONAL DRONES

by Matt Chandler

raintree

a Capstone company — publishers for children

Raintree is an imprint of Capstone Global Library Limited, a company incorporated in England and Wales having its registered office at 264 Banbury Road, Oxford, OX2 7DY – Registered company number: 6695582

www.raintree.co.uk
myorders@raintree.co.uk

Editorial Credits
Carrie Sheely, editor; Steve Mead, designer; Tracey Engel, media researcher; Katy LaVigne, production specialist

ISBN 978 1 4747 3315 1
20 19 18 17 16
10 9 8 7 6 5 4 3 2 1

British Library Cataloguing in Publication Data
A full catalogue record for this book is available from the British Library.

Acknowledgements
We would like to thank the following for permission to reproduce photographs:
123RF: modfos, 24; Alamy: Maurice Savage, 18, ZUMA Press, Inc., 27; AP Images: Peter Thomson/La Crosse Tribune, 25, Kamran Jebreili, 5; Getty Images: Ethan Miller/Staff, 6-7, Neo Chee Wei/Contributor, 14; iStockphoto: Franck-Boston, 16-17; Newscom: CHARLES PLATIAU/REUTERS, 20-21, CHINE NOUVELLE/SIPA/1509101149, 29; Shutterstock: Andis Rea, Design Element, Brothers Good, Cover and Interior Design Element, Chesky, Design Element, DamienGeso, Design Element, Fineart1, 13, Kolonkok, Design Element, Konstantin Ustinov, Design Element, LiliGraphie, Cover Background, Nik Merkulov, Cover and Interior Design Element, Pagina, Design Element, ProstoSvet, Front and Back Cover, robuart, Design Element, seregalsv, 8-9, SunnyStock, 11, Vjom, Cover and Interior Design Element; SuperStock: Alf Jönsson/imageBROKER, 23

Every effort has been made to contact copyright holders of material reproduced in this book. Any omissions will be rectified in subsequent printings if notice is given to the publisher.

All the internet addresses (URLs) given in this book were valid at the time of going to press. However, due to the dynamic nature of the internet, some addresses may have changed, or sites may have changed or ceased to exist since publication. While the author and publisher regret any inconvenience this may cause readers, no responsibility for any such changes can be accepted by either the author or the publisher.

Printed and bound in China.

CONTENTS

CHAPTER 1

DRONE FLYING FUN

Bonney Field in Sacramento, California, in the United States is usually home to football tournaments. But in the summer of 2015 during the state fair, the field was transformed into a flight zone. More than 100 drone pilots took part in the Fat Shark US National Drone Racing Championships. At first glance, it might have looked like the seated racers were just relaxing with friends. But upon a closer look, their goggles and slight, quick hand movements would have told a different story. These racers were locked in fierce competition while twisting their drones through a challenging course. In the end, Australian pilot Chad Nowak became the first US national champion.

Drones have been around for nearly 100 years. The first **recreational** drones were a **novelty** for many years. In the 1930s, they drew attention from just a small group of enthusiasts. Unlike today's battery-operated models, early drones ran on petrol. These bulky airplanes often had wingspans of more than 3 metres (10 feet).

recreational done for enjoyment, usually in people's spare time

novelty something new, interesting and unusual

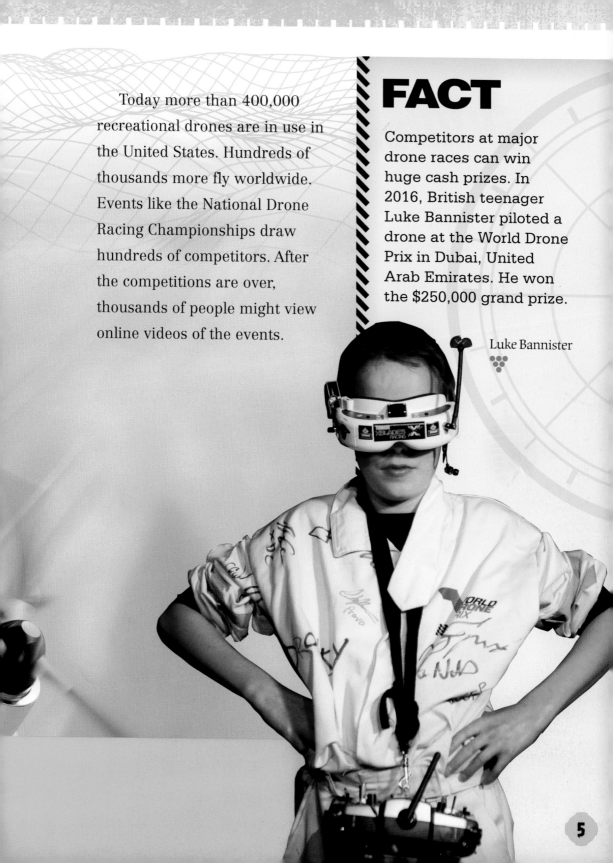

Today more than 400,000 recreational drones are in use in the United States. Hundreds of thousands more fly worldwide. Events like the National Drone Racing Championships draw hundreds of competitors. After the competitions are over, thousands of people might view online videos of the events.

FACT

Competitors at major drone races can win huge cash prizes. In 2016, British teenager Luke Bannister piloted a drone at the World Drone Prix in Dubai, United Arab Emirates. He won the $250,000 grand prize.

Luke Bannister

CHAPTER 2

CHOOSING A DRONE

Drones that fly are also called unmanned aerial vehicles (UAVs). All UAVs share some features. A pilot on the ground operates a UAV using a **remote control** device. Some UAVs also can fly on a pre-programmed flight path. Beyond that, each UAV has its own unique features and capabilities. Buyers choose recreational drones based on their own needs and preferences.

Parrot's Disco fixed-wing drone can fly at about 80 kilometres (50 miles) per hour.

Drones can have **rotors** or fixed wings. Quadcopters are one of the most common types of rotor drones. They have four rotors. Other recreational drones have six or eight rotors. The biggest difference in the number of rotors is the amount of **thrust** the drone can generate.

Fixed-wing drones don't have rotors. They look like small aeroplanes. These drones usually have a longer battery life than rotor drones do.

Some drones are even multi-purpose. Parrot's Hydrofoil drone can fly in the air. But it can also ride on the surface of the water. As a watercraft, it reaches a top speed of 10 kilometres (6 miles) per hour.

FACT

Axis Drones' Aerius mini-drone is so small it fits on the tip of a finger.

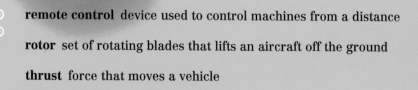

remote control device used to control machines from a distance

rotor set of rotating blades that lifts an aircraft off the ground

thrust force that moves a vehicle

DRONES FOR EVERY EXPERIENCE LEVEL

With so many choices available, buying a drone is no simple task. A beginner pilot may want an inexpensive drone that is easier to replace when it crashes. Beginners can buy a basic drone for as little as £20.

As pilots get better at flying, they can upgrade to more advanced flying machines. An experienced pilot may choose an octocopter. This type of drone has eight arms that each operate on an individual motor. Pilots can often attach large cameras to these strong drones.

DRONES FOR SPECIFIC PURPOSES

Before buying, hobbyists should consider how they will use the drone. Racers need a small drone with a lot of power, such as the OFM Seeker 450 V2 quadcopter. This drone can reach a top speed of 100 kilometres (62 miles) per hour. It is one of the fastest racing drones on the market today. Some racers have drones with carbon fibre frames. Carbon fibre is lightweight yet strong.

FACT

If one or two engines fail on an octocopter, the pilot can still land the drone with the remaining engines.

 An octocopter flies through the air holding a large camera.

DRONES FOR PHOTOGRAPHY

The ability to take stunning videos and photos is a main attraction for many drone enthusiasts. Drone cameras allow hobbyists to capture overhead shots of mountainous regions, forests and other areas. Buyers interested in photography should consider the quality of a drone's cameras. The quality of cameras on recreational drones varies. Some basic cameras have 2-**megapixel resolution**, while advanced cameras often have at least 10-megapixel resolution. Most drones also have **high-definition** (HD) video cameras.

Professional photographers often use the Phantom 3. This drone snaps 12-megapixel still photos. A wide-angle lens captures a large area to the sides. The drone also has image stabilization to reduce blurring. A control lets the pilot easily hover to take images.

FACT

In 2016, the Federal Aviation Administration (FAA) updated its rules for those who want to fly drones for business use in the United States. Pilots of drones weighing from 250 grams to 25 kilograms (0.55 to 55 pounds) must be at least 16 years old. They also need to complete training and get a certificate. These pilots also need to follow all of the FAA's other drone rules.

The DJI Phantom 3 can stay in the air for about 20 minutes before needing to be recharged.

 megapixel one million pixels; a pixel is a very small dot that makes up a picture on a TV screen, computer monitor or other digital device

resolution ability of a device to show an image clearly and with a lot of detail

high-definition having a high clarity of visual presentation; cameras labelled as HD meet certain resolution and other standards

CRASH CONSIDERATIONS

Drones are built to be lightweight and fast. However, these qualities also make drones vulnerable. Most popular recreational drones won't survive a crash from hundreds of metres in the air. Weather can easily cause a drone to crash. Even a light gust of wind can send a tiny drone off course. When purchasing a drone, buyers need to consider how well the drone will stand up to crashes.

Some manufacturers sell crash kits. These kits can come with everything from replacement propellers to a new body cover for the drone. Crash kits allow many repairs to be made in the field at a minimal cost.

Owners of more expensive drones may buy drone **insurance**. The insurance can cover some of the costs resulting from a crash.

FACT

The small Walkera QR Infra X Smart drone was the first to have a crash-avoidance system. If an object is nearby, it will automatically fly in the opposite direction.

 insurance agreement in which a person makes regular payments to a company and the company promises to pay money if the item insured is damaged or lost

Crashes can easily damage fragile parts such as propellers. Replacement propellers and other parts can be helpful to have on hand.

DIY DRONES

With so many types of drones available, there is a drone that fits the needs of almost every buyer. But some people want the challenge of building their own **custom** drones. These drone enthusiasts either use drone kits or build drones from scratch. Basic kits have everything needed to build a drone for less than £60.

A man gets ready to fly his home-made drone in a park in Singapore.

To build a drone from scratch, all the parts must be purchased individually. Building a custom drone in this way isn't for beginners. Like any complex machine, building a drone takes a lot of knowledge and patience. An understanding of **aerodynamics** is critical. The way a builder shapes a drone and positions the rotors will determine its success in flight. Knowledge of small-engine design can help hobbyists to build their own engines. Experience with **robotics** can lead to even more features. Imagine a drone with a robotic arm that can land and grab you a snack!

Experts say the advantage to building a drone is having a better understanding of how it works. Drones can be tricky to fly, and many inexperienced operators crash their drones. Building your own drone can lead to better piloting skills.

custom specially done or made

aerodynamics ability of something to move easily and quickly through the air

robotics field that deals with the design, construction and operation of robots

CHAPTER 3

GET BEHIND THE CONTROLS

Once you have a drone, it's time for the most exciting part – getting behind the controls! Children as young as seven can learn to fly a simple drone.

The handheld controller is the pilot's connection to the drone. Just like a video game controller, most recreational drone controllers have two joysticks. These are used to control the **pitch**, **yaw**, throttle and **roll** of the drone. The throttle determines how fast the drone travels. Once the drone is airborne, the pilot must maintain its height in the air while controlling the other elements.

One of the most important manoeuvres for a pilot to master is the roll. Many drone crashes happen when a pilot flies the drone into an object such as a building or tree. A roll can redirect the drone and avoid a crash.

pitch turn on an axis so that the forward end rises or falls in relation to the other end

yaw movement of an aircraft to the left or right

roll movement of an aircraft in a circular motion to the left or right

Many drones have a screen on the controller. This lets pilots see the view from the drone's camera.

KNOW THE RULES

Before you fly, there are some rules to know. The UK Civil Aviation Authority (CAA) states that drones cannot fly higher than 122 metres (400 feet). Drones should be kept away from aircraft, airports and small airfields. Drones must not fly over busy areas in major towns and cities or above concerts or large sports events.

Some pilots have reported drones flying within 30 metres (100 feet) of their planes. This close distance can lead to a collision.

KEEPING OTHERS SAFE

By following rules, you help to protect others. A recreational drone can weigh as much as 25 kilograms (55 pounds). That's enough to cause a commercial airliner to crash under certain conditions if the two aircraft collide. In 2015, the CAA reported 23 "near misses" between drones and commercial airlines in a six-month period.

The United Kingdom has also implemented some additional regulations to protect the public. Drones with cameras must avoid flying within 50 metres (164 feet) of people, vehicles, buildings or other structures. The operator must also be able to see the drone. People who want to use drones for business use must get permission from the CAA.

CHAPTER 4

RECREATIONAL DRONE USES

From racing to photography, the uses of recreational drones are many. Some people like to post selfies on social media to share with their friends. Thanks to drones, there is a new type of photo gaining popularity – the "dronie". To make one, fly your drone and snap a shot of yourself. Imagine how different you might look from 15 metres (50 feet) above the ground!

FIGHTING DRONES

Though it's still rare, some pilots take part in drone combat. The rules are simple: the last drone flying wins. Battle rules allow bumping the opponent's drone in an attempt to make it crash. Drone fights can sharpen the skills of pilots. To escape an attack drone, a pilot might need to make several quick dives or turns. In the US, a combat drone group called Game of Drones holds events in the San Francisco area that draw hundreds of spectators.

FACT

Hundreds of drone clubs operate around the world. By joining a club, pilots can share their hobby with others and learn more about drones.

Drone enthusiasts gather at the Intergalactic Meeting of Phantom's Pilots in Paris, France, in 2014.

RACING DRONES

As drones have become more popular, drone racing has become more organized.

For most races, competitors race around a marked course for a certain number of laps. The racer with the fastest time wins. Classes are often divided up based on the type of drone being flown. Other races are based on a points system. Racers earn points for finishing each **heat** under a set amount of time. The racer with the most points after a certain number of heats wins. Racers often need to qualify for championship events by winning in smaller events.

DRONE RACING LEAGUE

The Drone Racing League is a large competitive racing group that draws pilots from around the world. The league holds events throughout the United States. Pilots are ranked nationally in standings. In 2016, the group held a race inside Sun Life Stadium in Miami, Florida, USA. The stadium is home to the Miami Dolphins American football club.

 heat single round of a contest

Thanks to first-person-view (FPV) flying, racers can feel as though they are in the cockpit of the drone. The drone camera relays real-time video back to a pair of goggles worn by the pilot.

FACT

Many racers add neon lights to their racing drones. This makes the drones more visible for race spectators.

A racer uses FPV goggles to fly his drone.

PUTTING DRONES TO WORK

Recreational drones are made to fly for fun. But that doesn't mean they can't be used for purposeful work. If a homeowner has a leak in the attic, he or she may have to climb onto the roof to inspect the damage. This can be dangerous. Instead, the homeowner can fly a drone over the house and photograph the roof. The owner can then instantly see the damage without ever leaving the ground.

Gardeners can use drones to inspect their gardens and identify areas that need attention. This can be especially helpful in rural areas where gardens can be quite large.

Drones can help workers and homeowners to inspect rooftops safely.

DRONES FOR POLICE USE

You might be used to seeing police officers chasing suspects on TV. But imagine a suspect being chased by a drone! Law enforcement agencies are just one of many groups using recreational drones for business use. Police in Mesa County, Colorado, were some of the first officers to use drones in the United States. The drones have logged more than 300 hours of flight time and have been on more than 80 missions. Police use the drones to track suspects and re-create crime scenes, as well as for other jobs.

CHAPTER 5

THE FUTURE OF RECREATIONAL DRONES

Recreational drone use shows no signs of slowing down. The FAA predicts that by 2020 there will be 4.3 million recreational drones in the United States alone. Add to that several million commercial drones and the skies will be crowded. With this increase, new laws are likely to come. These laws can help to protect people from injury and help ensure people's privacy.

In recent years drone manufacturers have partnered to help promote drone use and fair laws for them. In 2016, some leading drone manufacturers formed the Drone Manufacturers Alliance. The members of the group include DJI, 3D Robotics, GoPro and Parrot. The group wants to promote laws that allow the safe use of drones. They also want to promote creative design in drone manufacturing.

CHECKING LOCAL LAWS

Drone owners need to know laws specific to where they are flying. Both national and local laws may change depending on the area. For example, the FAA has stricter guidelines in the Washington DC area for national defence reasons. In 2015, a recreational drone user was flying a drone at night. He lost control of the quadcopter. He knew the drone would soon run out of battery life. He thought it would crash nearby, so he didn't go to look for it right away. But the next day he learned it had crashed at the White House. Despite his mistake, he was not charged with a crime.

Drone manufacturers will continue to push the limits with new drone technology and capabilities. Object avoidance is one area of drone technology manufacturers are trying to improve. In 2016, two researchers at Stanford University in California made a drone that can dodge the quick jabs of a fencing sword. Improvements in this area can help drones to travel more safely. In contrast, the Gimball rescue drone is designed to survive bumping into objects. This rescue drone won the Drones for Good international competition in 2015. Its robust design will allow it to bounce off objects while searching for victims in remote areas.

The use of cutting-edge technology will increase the choices on offer to people wanting to buy drones. These advancements will also help to expand the types of jobs drones can do. From inspections in factories to making life-saving deliveries, the possibilities for drones seem endless.

A woman displays the Gimball drone at a World Economic Forum meeting in China in 2015.

FACT

In 2015, the first International Drone Day events were held. Organizers formed the events to help to promote the benefits of drone use.

GLOSSARY

aerodynamics the ability of something to move easily and quickly through the air

custom specially done or made

high definition having a high clarity of visual presentation; cameras labelled as HD meet a certain resolution standard and other requirements

heat single round of a contest

insurance agreement in which a person makes regular payments to a company and the company promises to pay money if the item insured is damaged or lost

megapixel one million pixels; a pixel is a very small dot that makes up a picture on a TV screen, computer monitor or other digital device

novelty something new, interesting and unusual

pitch turn on an axis so that the forward end rises or falls in relation to the other end

recreational done for enjoyment, usually in people's spare time

remote control device used to control machines from a distance

resolution ability of a device to show an image clearly and with a lot of detail

robotics field that deals with the design, construction and operation of robots

roll movement of an aircraft in a circular motion to the left or right

rotor set of rotating blades that lifts an aircraft off the ground

thrust force that moves a vehicle

yaw movement of an aircraft to the left or right

READ MORE

Drones (Beginners Plus), Henry Brook (Usborne Publishing, 2016)

Drones: An Illustrated Guide to the Unmanned Aircraft That Are Filling Our Skies, Martin J. Dougherty (Amber Books, 2015)

The Complete Guide to Drones, Adam Juniper (Ilex Press, 2015)

WEBSITES

bmfa.org/multi-rotors
The British Model Flying Association has information on the legal requirements for flying recreational drones and gives guidance on flying them safely.

www.caa.co.uk/droneaware
Check out the Civil Aviation Authority website for drone laws and safety guides.

INDEX